Roger's Long Ride

I Talk You Talk Press

CONTENTS

I Talk You Talk Press

1. A BAD WEEK

Roger grew up in Medford in Oregon. He loved food and cooking, so after high school he studied to be a chef. He worked in restaurants and cafes in Medford, but his dream was to live in a big city.

I'd like to work in San Francisco. I would learn a lot about food and cooking there. I might become a famous chef, he thought. *Maybe I could have my own restaurant one day.*

Finally, he got a job in a small café in the Mission District of San Francisco. He found a furnished room in an apartment less than a mile from the café. His roommates were Cameron and Oliver. They were brothers. They had lived in San Francisco for a long time. They were truck drivers. When he went to look at the apartment, Cameron said, "Our family has a hardware store in Chico. Our father wants help. Our brother Otis has gone home to work in the store. The rent of this apartment is too much for Oliver and me, so we need a roommate. You can have Otis' room if you want it."

Roger liked living with Cameron and Oliver. He liked his work at the café. Marietta was one of the waitresses at the café. She was very pretty. Roger liked her very much. After a few months, they started dating.

Marietta loved going to the beach. Roger saved some money and borrowed some more money from the bank to buy a car. When they had a day off work, Roger and Marietta drove to the beach and watched the sunset.

Life was good.

Then Covid 19 came. Many people got sick. Some people died.

Everyone wore masks and tried to stay home. A few months later, Roger's life changed.

One Monday, Roger's boss said, "I have to close the café. It is impossible. People are staying home. No one goes to cafes anymore. I lose money every day. I will pay you for today, but I'm sorry. This is the end of your job with me. You are a good worker. If things get better, I will ask you to come back."

On Tuesday, Roger went to the café to collect his money and his chef's knives. Marietta was there. She had lost her job too, but she wasn't unhappy.

"I'm going home to New Mexico," she said. "My parents are telling me I must start planning for my wedding."

"Wedding!" Roger was amazed. *I didn't ask Marietta to marry me,* he thought.

"Yes." Marietta was smiling. "I am going to marry my boyfriend from high school. He has a good job now, so we can get married."

"But what about us?" Roger was shouting. "You never told me about this other guy! I thought I was your boyfriend."

Marietta kissed him on the cheek. "I wanted to have some fun before I got married. You were my California boyfriend. You're very nice, but I was never serious about you."

Roger left the café and walked to a park. He was shocked and unhappy. He sat in the park for hours. Finally, it got cold, and Roger realised he was hungry.

I'll go back to the apartment and cook something delicious for dinner. Cameron and Oliver like my food.

As Roger walked along Bryant Street towards the apartment he saw a big truck driving away from the apartment building. *That's strange,* he thought. *That looks like Cameron's truck. He should be out delivering food to supermarkets on the other side of the city.*

He climbed the stairs to the apartment and unlocked the door. He could not believe what he saw inside. The apartment was empty! All the furniture had gone!

Someone has come here and stolen everything! I must call the police!

He ran to his bedroom. All the furniture was gone, but his blankets were folded up in a corner. His pillows were on top of the blankets. His laptop, books and clothes were in another corner and his bicycle was leaning against the wall. *Who steals the furniture and leaves a computer?* he asked himself.

Then his phone rang. He opened it. There was a text from Cameron.

---Hi Roger.

Oliver and I are sorry. We got a call this morning from Otis. Mom and Dad have Covid 19. They are very ill and they are in hospital. Maybe Dad will die. We're on our way back to Chico to be with them, and to help Otis with the store. We don't think we will come back to San Francisco for a long time. So we have taken everything with us. The rent is paid until the end of this month. Maybe you can find new roommates. You are a good guy, and we hate doing this to you. If you are ever in Chico, be sure to come and visit us. Good luck.---

Roger sat on the floor. *This is not their fault,* he thought. *They didn't want to do this to me.*

He sent a text to Cameron.

---Sorry to read about your parents. I hope they will be well soon. Don't worry about me.---

Roger was very hungry. He went to the kitchen. The refrigerator was gone. The table was gone. His pots and dishes were on the counter. They were all filled with food.

He ate some bread and cheese.

I must decide what to do. I borrowed money to buy the car. But I will have no money now to pay the bank. I must sell my car. I have no furniture. I have no money to pay the rent. I must leave this apartment. Where can I go? What can I do?

Roger looked at the pile of pots and frying pan. The only other thing left in the kitchen was a calendar. The picture on the calendar was of a young boy. His clothes were old and dirty, but he had a big smile on his face. He was standing next to a table with a jug, a pile of lemons and some old glasses. A little sign said 'lemonade 5 cents a glass'. And across the bottom of the picture was a message. 'When life gives you lemons – make lemonade'.

Life has given me lemons this week, thought Roger. *I have lost my job, my apartment and my girlfriend. I must sell my car.*

Then he had an idea. Make lemonade! He sat on the floor and called his cousin Kurt in Medford. When Kurt answered, he said, "Hi Kurt. This is Roger. How are you?"

"I'm fine."

"How is your family?"

"Everyone is good. It's nice to hear from you. But how are you? Are you OK?"

"Yes, no. It's been a bad week."

"A bad week? Roger, it's only Tuesday today!"

"I'll tell you later," said Roger. "I have a question. Is my old van still in the garage at your parents' house?"

"Sure. It's yours. Why?"

"I have an idea. I want to come back to Medford. I want to turn my old van into a food truck! What do you think? You are very good at working on cars and trucks. Can you help me?"

"Mmm." Kurt was thinking. "Yes, I think so. I feel like doing something new. If you make me a partner, I will do the work for free. But we will need money to pay for materials and equipment."

"I'll sell my car," said Roger. "I will have to pay back the money I borrowed from the bank. But I will still have maybe three thousand dollars. Will that be enough?"

"Maybe," said Kurt. "In two weeks I can take a vacation. We can make a plan and start working on the van. It will be great! Can you be here in two weeks?"

"Yes. I can leave San Francisco this week. I'll see you soon."

Roger was feeling much better. *I have a plan! I have a business partner.* He took the calendar down from the wall. *I'll take this with me, so that I can remember.*

A few minutes later, Roger got a text from Kurt.

---Sell your car in San Francisco. You will get more money there.---

How can I get to Medford? I could take a bus. No. I have a lot of time. Kurt won't be free for two weeks. I'll use a moving company to send most of my things to Medford and I'll ride my bicycle! It will be a vacation.

2. FIONNA

Three days later, Roger was riding through Petaluma, looking for somewhere to stop and have a picnic lunch. His bicycle started to make a strange noise. There was something in the front wheel. He stopped outside an old building and looked.

That's no problem. It's a small stick. Maybe I picked it up when I was riding through the park, he thought.

He lifted his bike onto the sidewalk, and leant it against the wall of a building. He knelt down on the ground to fix the problem. Then he heard a voice.

"Excuse me."

He looked around. The street was empty.

"Excuse me," said the voice again. "I'm up here."

Roger looked up. There was a woman leaning out of a window on the second floor of the building.

"Can you help me please?"

Roger looked up at the woman.

"How can I help you?"

"I can't go to the supermarket, and I need food. If I pay you, will you go to the supermarket for me?"

"Why can't you go to the supermarket?"

"If I leave the apartment, the men from the city will come. They will lock the doors. I won't be able to get inside. There will be no one to look after my cats. They will die. I have to stay here."

"What about your neighbours? Can they help you?"

"There are no neighbours now. Everyone left last week."

I don't understand, thought Roger. He looked at the building. The name sign said 'Caledonia Apartments'. It was old. There were no curtains at the windows. Then he saw a big notice.

---*'Safety Hazard. Danger. Do not enter. This building is not safe.'*---

Why is she here? I think she is a little crazy. But I will go to the supermarket for her, and I will find someone to help her, thought Roger.

"Uh. OK," he said. "What do you want?"

"Please wait," said the woman. She disappeared from the window.

Roger fixed his bicycle while he was waiting.

"Coming down now!" said the woman.

Roger looked up. A basket was coming down from the window. It was on a piece of rope.

He caught the basket and looked inside. There was a plastic bag with a shopping list and $75. He took the bag.

"OK," he said. "I'll go to the supermarket for you."

"Thank you!" shouted the woman, and she pulled the basket back up to her window.

Roger rode to the nearest supermarket. He put everything on the list into a shopping cart – cans of tuna fish, bottles of water, milk, tea, bread, cat food, tomatoes, mayonnaise…

This is only enough for a few days, he thought. *I must do something to help her. It might be many days until someone stops outside her building again.*

Roger looked at the checkout operators. He chose an older woman. *Maybe she knows this neighbourhood. Maybe she knows the woman I talked to.*

While the woman was scanning the items, Roger said, "This shopping is for a woman who lives in Caledonia Apartments. Do you know that building?"

The checkout operator looked at the cat food, milk and cans of tuna. "Fionna! Is she still there?"

"I don't know her name. But she asked me to help her."

There were people standing behind Roger at the checkout. The woman looked at her watch. "My name is Anna. I want to talk to you. I have my afternoon coffee break in five minutes. Please wait outside."

Roger paid for the shopping and carried the bags outside.

Very soon Anna came out of the supermarket.

"Let's sit over there." She pointed to an outdoor café. "Do you want something to drink?"

"No thanks," said Roger. "I'm fine."

"I don't know you," said Anna. "Why are you shopping for Fionna?"

Roger told Anna about his bicycle ride. He told her what happened outside Caledonia Apartments. "I didn't know what to do. I thought, 'first I must buy her some food, and then find someone to help her'."

"We call Fionna 'the cat lady'," said Anna. "She is alone. She has five cats. Her cats are her children. When the engineers said the building was not safe, the city government found new apartments for all the people who lived there.

"But the new apartments all have a rule – 'no pets'. So Fionna wouldn't move to a new apartment. But I know that now there is no electricity and no water in the Caledonia Apartment building. And it's not safe. The building might fall down! This is not good! I must think of something. Fionna is a little crazy, but she is a good woman and she is alone."

Anna's coffee came and she took off her mask to drink it. "Please wait," she said. "I'm thinking. I must find someone whom Fionna trusts."

Roger was worried. "I must go back soon. Fionna gave me money. Maybe she will think I took the money and went away!"

"Hmm," said Anna. "I have an idea."

She took out her phone. "I am going to call my cousin. She goes to the same church as Fionna."

Roger waited while Anna talked on the phone. She talked for a long time.

When she finished her call, she smiled. "My cousin knows Fionna well. She has a farm about thirty miles north of here. There is a small house on the farm. She says Fionna and her cats can stay there. She is in town today. She will come and meet you at the apartment building. I must go back to work."

Roger rode back to the apartment building. Fionna was looking out of the window. She lowered the basket on the rope. Roger put the shopping in a few items at a time. Fionna pulled the basket up and emptied it. Then, she let it down again.

Finally, he put the receipt from the supermarket and the change from the $75 in the basket.

Fionna shouted to him. "I must pay you. There is forty dollars change. Please keep it."

"No! I don't want you to pay me," shouted Roger.

Just then a truck stopped next to him.

A small woman in a baseball cap jumped out. "Hi Fionna," she shouted. "It's me, Meggie."

Fionna looked surprised. "Meggie? What are you doing here?"

"Wallace, one of my farm workers, retired. He has gone to Arizona. His cottage is empty. Why don't you come and stay there? This building is not safe. You have no water or electricity. The cottage is small, but it will be much better."

"But my cats! I can't leave my cats!"

"If you stay here, the building might fall down. It is too dangerous for your cats. They might die. Come to the farm. Your cats can come too."

"Uh, OK. I hope my cats will like the farm."

"Do you need help?" Roger called out. "Can I carry things to the truck for you?"

It took a long time.

Meggie helped Fionna pack. Roger climbed up and down the stairs. He carried many things to the truck. Cat baskets, cat cages, all the food he had bought at the supermarket, suitcases, books....

Finally, everything was finished.

He waved to Fionna as Meggie drove away.

I was going to ride to Santa Rosa today, but I am too tired. It doesn't matter. I will ride a long way tomorrow. I will look on my phone and find a campground here in Petaluma.

3. A SURPRISE VISITOR

Roger left Petaluma at 8:30am. The trip from Petaluma to Butte City took a long time. Roger stopped for drinks and snacks, and it was almost 8:30pm when he arrived at the campground next to the lake in Butte City.

It was a beautiful area. He paid for a place for his tent in a camping area close to the lake. He chained his bicycle to a fence. It was late, and he was tired. So he heated a can of beans on his camping stove and drank a bottle of beer.

He was looking at the lake. *This is so quiet and peaceful,* he thought. *I am tired. I will go to sleep soon. Tomorrow I will ride to Chico. I will visit Cameron and Oliver. I hope their parents are OK.*

He tidied up his campsite. He took his towel and some clean clothes and walked over to the shower and toilet building at the campsite. When he came out of the shower building, it was dark. He turned on his torch, so he could see his way.

When he crawled into his tent, he got a big surprise. There was someone in the tent! A young woman was sitting on the ground.

He stared at her. She was very thin. She was wearing a handkerchief instead of a mask, so he couldn't see her face. But she had long blonde hair and pale blue eyes. Her clothes were strange. She was wearing overalls and a man's shirt.

"Why are you in my tent?" he asked.

"Please," whispered the young woman. "Please be quiet. I am hiding. They will find me! That's why I got into your tent."

Roger didn't know what to do. "Who is looking for you?" he

asked.

She didn't answer his question. "Please let me stay here. I am very frightened."

"Are the police looking for you?" asked Roger.

"No! No! I am not hiding from the police."

"Then if you are frightened, I will call the police," said Roger. He took his phone from his pocket.

"Please, no! Don't call the police. Please let me stay here tonight."

Roger didn't know what to do. It was late and he was tired. "OK," he said. "I will take my sleeping bag. I will sleep outside. You can stay here."

The next morning, Roger woke up very early. He was cold and stiff from sleeping on the ground.

He walked back to his tent. He looked at the fence. *My bike has gone! Someone has stolen my bike!*

He opened the tent flap and looked inside. The woman had gone. There was a piece of paper on the floor of the tent. She had written one word. —-'Sorry'—

I was an idiot! I left my backpack with my keys, my credit cards and my money in the tent. Roger looked inside his wallet. *My credit cards are here. I had $520, but now I only have $500. She took $20.* Roger thought it was very strange. *Why didn't she take all my money?*

Everything else was in the tent. The strange woman had taken his bicycle, his helmet and $20.

What shall I do now? I could take a bus to Chico.

Roger called Cameron.

"How are your parents?" he asked.

"Their health is much better," said Cameron. "Our mother is home from the hospital. She is staying with her sister. Our father is still in hospital, but his condition is not dangerous. Thank you for asking. When Otis called to say Mom and Dad had Covid 19, and were in hospital, Oliver and I panicked. Later, we felt very bad that we walked out on you. Are you OK?"

"Yes, I'm OK. I'm going back to Medford. I am at the campground in Butte City."

"That's only twenty miles from here. You must come to visit us. You must stay with us." Cameron sounded excited.

"Thank you," said Roger. "I would like to do that. Someone stole my bike, but maybe I can take a bus."

"Take a bus! Are you crazy? Stay where you are. I am coming to get you."

Cameron arrived an hour later in a small van. The sign on the van said 'Greenway Hardware'.

Roger had packed everything, so very soon Cameron was driving back to Chico with Roger's bags in the back of the van.

"Tell me what happened," said Cameron. "Tell me everything."

Roger told Cameron about losing his job, about Marietta breaking up with him, about Fionna, and about the strange woman in his tent. "She found my bike keys. She took my bike, my helmet and $20," he said.

Cameron laughed. Roger felt angry. "I don't think it's funny," he said.

Cameron was still laughing. "Yes it is!" he said. "You are amazing! Your life is terrible, but you said, 'I am OK'."

Roger thought about what Cameron had said. Then he laughed too. "I guess it is funny. So many things have gone wrong in my life so quickly, but I met Fionna and I could help her. And I met Anna and Meggie. They are kind people."

Cameron patted Roger's knee. "That's true. But you are a kind person too. You are a good guy. So now the Greenway family is going to help you."

4. THE GREENWAY FAMILY

Cameron drove into Chico. He drove up to a big house in a nice suburb.

Roger was nervous. "Your father is in hospital. I can't stay here. Please take me to a camping ground."

"No way! You are our friend. You will stay with us. You can cook for us. Our Mom will be pleased. She is worried because we are only eating frozen pizzas and takeaways."

Roger laughed. "OK. Thank you. I can stay for a few days."

"Why don't you stay longer? We are busy at the hardware store. We have staff but we need more people. Many people are staying home. They are bored. So they want to paint fences and fix things in their houses. They call or go online to make an order. We are delivering items from the shop all over the city. You won't need to cook all day. You can drive a van for us. We can pay you."

"My cousin Kurt expects me in about ten days' time. So I will look for a new bike and leave here in about one week. Is that OK?"

"It's great." Cameron took Roger into the house and showed him a spare bedroom. "You have your own bathroom," he said and pointed to a door in the bedroom. "Make yourself at home. Take anything you want."

Cameron went into another room. After a few minutes he came back with a key ring. "I called Mom. She is very pleased you are here. She was angry with Oliver and me because we emptied the apartment and walked out on you. She's also pleased because you can cook.

"These are the keys to the house and the keys for my Mom's little car. She said 'please tell Roger to use my car'. I have to go back to the shop now. See you later."

Roger heard Cameron drive away in the van. He made the bed in the spare room and took a shower. Then he found the kitchen. It was a mess. There were pizza boxes and beer bottles on the table. The garbage can was full of bags from a takeaway café. The dishwasher was full of dirty plates and coffee cups.

I think they need me here, thought Roger. *Cameron and Oliver were never so untidy in San Francisco.* He cleaned the kitchen. Then he opened the refrigerator. There was a terrible smell. The milk and vegetables were all bad. He found garbage bags and emptied the refrigerator.

He looked in the freezer. There was a lot of meat. He took out a large piece of beef. *I'll defrost this and cook it tonight. I need to buy vegetables, fruit and milk.*

He found a small supermarket near the house and bought fresh food.

Otis, Cameron and Oliver came back late.

Roger had cooked a pot roast with mashed potatoes and green beans. Oliver took a photograph of his meal with his phone. "I'll send this to Mom. She can stop worrying about whether we are eating properly!"

Otis, Cameron and Oliver enjoyed the food very much. They ate a lot.

"We are so busy!" said Otis. "It's crazy. Cameron said you lost your job. But you said you will only stay one week. Stay longer and work for us! You are a great cook and you can work maybe four hours a day in the store."

Roger looked around the table. He liked the Greenway brothers very much. "It is a good idea, but I have a plan. I have an old van in Medford. My cousin Kurt is great with cars and vans. I am going to turn my van into a food truck. Kurt will be my partner. What do you think?"

"It's a great plan," said Oliver. "You are an excellent chef. You don't want to be a delivery driver when you can make people happy with your food. You can take your food truck to the beach in summer and to baseball games. In winter you can take it to football games!"

Cameron was still eating, but he stopped and asked, "Will you sell hot dogs?"

"I don't think so. Many people sell hot dogs. I thought maybe I could sell good coffee, tacos and fancy sandwiches. I don't have a menu yet."

The four young men had a great evening. They talked about Roger's plans. They drank beer and watched a baseball game on television. Then it was time to go to bed.

"We have to start early in the hardware store," said Otis. The brothers stood up.

"Goodnight," said Otis. "Thank you for the great meal."

"I am so tired," laughed Oliver. "I ate too much."

"Goodnight," said Cameron. "What will you cook for breakfast? I like hotcakes and sausages."

Roger cleaned the kitchen and loaded the dishwasher before he went to bed.

5. IT WAS THE SAME GIRL!

Roger made French toast and bacon for breakfast. He made sandwiches for the brothers to eat at lunchtime.

"I can come and help you today," he said. "What do you want me to do?"

"Can you make deliveries for us?" asked Otis.

"Sure," said Roger. "I'll come to the store soon."

Roger enjoyed driving the van. It had GPS, so he could find his way easily. Everyone was trying to stay away from other people. So, at most houses, he drove up to the house and pressed the horn of the van. When he saw someone was home, he waved and put the order outside the house. Then he drove away.

Late in the day, Roger left the van at the store and drove Mrs Greenway's little car to the small supermarket. He planned to make Italian-style chicken with tomatoes and olives. He wanted to buy Italian cheese and green vegetables for salad.

Roger went to look at the vegetables. He was surprised. The shelves were almost empty.

"You don't have any vegetables today! Yesterday you had a lot."

The man at the checkout was old. His name tag said 'Winston'. "This is my store," he said. "All my staff are much younger than me, but they are sick with Covid 19. I have some boxes of vegetables and fruit outside. They are heavy, and I can't carry them."

"I can help you," smiled Roger. "Where are your vegetables?"

"I buy them from a vegetable farm. They bring them into Chico and put them in a shed behind the store. Can you bring them in, and help me put them on the shelves?"

"Sure," said Roger. He carried the boxes into the store. He helped Winston put lettuces, kale, cabbages, tomatoes, onions and leeks onto the shelves.

When they were finished, Winston said, "Thank you very much. I will pay you."

"No, no!" said Roger. "I was happy to help."

He chose some salad ingredients and found the cheese he wanted. He went to the checkout to pay for the cheese and the vegetables. He couldn't see Winston's mouth because he was wearing a mask, but his eyes looked angry. "Did you come in that car?" He pointed to Mrs Greenway's little car. It was the only car in the parking lot.

"Yes, that's right," answered Roger. "Why?"

Winston looked angry. "That is Ada Greenway's car! She has been sick. She is staying with her sister. You stole her car!"

"I didn't! I am staying at her house. She said I could drive her car."

"I don't believe you! I will call the police!"

Roger was worried. "Do you know Otis, Cameron and Oliver?" he asked.

"Of course I do. Usually Ada does all the food shopping, but recently they have been coming here to buy frozen pizzas and beer."

"If you want to call the police, that's OK. But please call the hardware store first. Talk to one of the boys. They will tell you about me."

Winston was not happy, but he walked away from the checkout counter and made the phone call. He talked a lot and looked at Roger. When he came back, his eyes were happy again.

"Otis said everything is fine. You are helping them with deliveries and you are cooking for them. Did you buy enough food? Those Greenway boys eat a lot!"

He put Roger's shopping into a bag and added a big container of ice cream and some packets of snacks.

"Sorry, I didn't believe you," he said. "The ice cream and the snacks are a present from me."

"It's OK," said Roger. "I think it is a good thing that you care for your customers."

He went out to the parking lot and put his shopping in the car. He was going to drive away when he thought, *Did I close the door of the shed? I can't remember.*

He hurried behind the supermarket. The shed door was open. *It's lucky I remembered,* he thought. He was walking towards the door when someone ran out of the shed!

Roger was amazed. It was the woman who stole his bicycle!

"Hey!" he shouted. "Stop!"

He was too late. The woman ran very fast. She climbed over a fence and disappeared.

When they were eating that night, Roger told the Greenway brothers about the young woman who ran out of the shed.

"It was the same woman," he said. "The woman who was hiding in my tent in Butte City. I am sure."

"I think you made a mistake," said Cameron. "Why do you think it was the same woman? Why do you think it was the woman who stole your bike, your helmet and $20?"

"Her long blonde hair. It is so pale, it is almost white. And her strange clothes. I am sure it is the same person."

"I have an idea," said Otis. "Mom and Dad opened the hardware store more than forty years ago. They know many people in this area. Maybe they know a family with very blonde hair. I think we should talk to them. If they know the family, you can call the police."

Roger said, "I think she is in trouble. I think she is very frightened. I'm not thinking about the police. I'm thinking about helping her."

"Roger, the romantic," shouted Oliver.

"Roger's in love!" Cameron was laughing.

Then Cameron stopped laughing. "Maybe Roger is right," he said. "I feel bad when I think of a young woman who is frightened."

"It is too late to call Mom or Dad tonight," said Otis. "But tomorrow I will call them. Maybe they can help."

6. CAREY-LOU

The next morning, Roger cooked breakfast, made box lunches and tidied the house.

"I'll call you when we have deliveries," said Otis.

Roger made coffee and sat at the kitchen table. *There was something strange yesterday,* he thought. *What was it?*

Then he remembered.

Roger drove to the supermarket. There was a young man on the checkout looking at his phone. "Is Winston here?" asked Roger.

"Sure. He's in the store somewhere." The young man went back to looking at his phone.

Roger found Winston. "I'm pleased you have some help today," he said.

"Yes. My grandson, Cassidy. He's lazy, but he's better than no staff at all. How can I help you?"

"I was thinking about yesterday. Your storage shed wasn't locked. I'm surprised. Why don't you lock the shed?"

Winston looked embarrassed. "Usually I lock the shed. I save all the boxes that the food for the store is delivered in. There is a big pile of boxes next to the shed. When I have enough, I call the recyclers and they come and get them. But the day before yesterday, I took some empty boxes out. I thought someone was sleeping there. I saw a bed from some old cardboard boxes. I thought 'Covid times are very hard. Maybe someone has lost their job. I will leave the storage shed open.' I don't mind if a homeless person takes an apple or a lettuce. It's OK."

"You are a very kind man," said Roger. "I think a young woman is hiding near here. I saw her yesterday. She is very frightened."

He went to the hardware store. Cameron had a list of orders for him to deliver.

"Did Otis talk to your Mom and Dad?" asked Roger.

"I think so. But we are very busy today. I don't know what they said," answered Cameron.

In the evening, after everyone had eaten, Roger asked Otis, "Did you talk to your parents? What did they say?"

"They were very interested in your story. There is a community that lives in the hills near Butte City. The community is called Trayducket. Our Mom says they have different ideas about how to live. They don't believe in doctors or schools or banks. They don't pay taxes. No schools, no hospitals. They don't like strangers. No one knows much about these families. They all say their family name is Smith, but nobody thinks that is true. Sometimes they come to Chico to buy supplies. The important thing is that Mom says some of the people who live in that community have very light blonde hair and very pale blue eyes."

"Yes!" said Roger. "She has very big, pale blue eyes. She must be from that family!"

Just then Otis' phone rang. He went to another room to answer it.

When he came back, he looked very serious.

"That was Mom. She was telling her sister about your story. Aunt Rose says she saw some people from Trayducket in Chico today. They seemed to be looking for something."

"Or someone?" Roger was worried.

"Yes. Maybe they are looking for your mystery woman. Aunt Rose says that if she is frightened and hiding, we must do something to help her."

"We can call the police," said Oliver.

"I don't think so," answered Otis. "We are only guessing. We don't know how old she is. We don't know her name. I don't think the police can do anything. There are groups who help women who have trouble at home, but she will have to go to them. Otherwise they can't help her."

"I'll call Winston," said Cameron. "I will tell him the story. I will tell him what we think. He can watch. If he sees her, he can call you. I'll give him your phone number."

Roger couldn't sleep. He got up very early. He drove towards the little supermarket, and parked Mrs Greenway's car in a nearby street.

The store wasn't open, but Winston was inside. He opened the door when he saw Roger. "Come in! I haven't seen anyone. But I thought I heard the shed door open and close. I have some more vegetables coming today. Meggie will want to put them in the shed. I hope she doesn't frighten your mystery woman. She might run away."

"Meggie? You buy vegetables from a woman called Meggie?"

"Yes. Her farm is far from here, but she has low prices and her vegetables are always good. Why do you want to know?"

"I met a woman called Meggie in Petaluma a few days ago. Maybe it is the same person. Can I stay behind the store and watch for a while?"

"Sure. I will open the store soon. I will have no time to watch," said Winston.

Roger opened the door at the back of the store very quietly. He went outside and listened. *I can't see or hear anyone. But there are many old boxes. Maybe she is hiding behind them,* he thought.

"Hello!" he called out softly. "I met you in Butte City. You stayed in my tent. Don't be frightened. I only want to help you."

He heard a small sound. *Yes she's there,* he thought.

"I know you're hiding. Please come out. I'm your friend."

He started to walk towards the pile of boxes. "Don't come near me! Please! I'm sorry about your bike! And I took some money. You will bring the police!" She sounded very scared.

"I would like to get my bike and helmet back," said Roger. "But the money doesn't matter. Do you want some more money?"

There was no answer. Roger tried again. "Do you come from Trayducket? Some people from Trayducket were here in Chico yesterday. Maybe they are looking for you."

"Oh no! They'll find me! They'll take me back. I have to get away!"

"Don't panic. I'll think of something. I won't let them find you. Why did you run away? Why are they looking for you? What's your name?"

"My name is Carey-Lou Smith. My grandfather is the leader of everyone in Trayducket. He doesn't like anyone to leave. A few years ago, my mother helped me get away. I stayed with her sister in

Sacramento for two years. I went to school. I had a normal life. But then my mother died, and the men from Trayducket came and took me back. Now my grandfather says I must marry my cousin. He is forty years old. He's horrible! I hate him. So I ran away."

A truck came into the parking lot and turned towards the shed. "It's them! They've found me! I must go!" Carey-Lou was crying.

"No! No! Be quiet!" whispered Roger. "Stay there. Stay behind the boxes. Don't move."

7. ESCAPE!

The truck stopped and a woman climbed out. She was the same woman Roger had met in Petaluma. Winston came out of the back door of the store and Meggie said, "I brought everything on your order. Do you have someone to help me put the boxes in the shed?"

"I'll help," said Roger.

Meggie looked at Roger. "You're the young man who helped Fionna! How are you?"

"I'm very well, thank you," answered Roger. "How is Fionna?"

"She is very happy. Her cats like the cottage, and they like the farm."

Winston opened the shed door. "I have to go back to the store. My lazy grandson didn't come today."

Winston went away. Then an old truck stopped in the parking lot. Three men got out. They walked towards Roger and Meggie. They all had long hair and beards. They were wearing big boots and hats. They were not wearing masks. Roger was shocked. One of the men had very pale hair and very pale blue eyes.

Oh no! They mustn't find Carey-Lou!

The men pushed past Meggie and Roger. They went into the storage shed. "Wait!" shouted Meggie. "You can't do that!"

The men ignored her.

Soon they came back. "There's no one hiding there," said one of the men. "We'll look in this truck. Maybe she is hiding there."

"I know you, Hiram Smith! You won't search my truck! Who do you think you are?" Meggie was very angry. "I'll call the police!"

The men went towards Meggie's truck. Roger had an idea. "Please let them look," he whispered to Meggie. "They won't find anyone. And maybe you can help a young woman."

"They are looking for a young woman? OK. These men are not nice people. I will help."

Roger took his phone from his pocket. He sent a text to Cameron.

---*We need help. Trayducket men at Winston's store.*---

Then he sent a text to Winston.

---*In five minutes, please make a lot of noise. Say someone is stealing food from your store.*---

A few minutes later, the men climbed down from the truck and walked towards Meggie and Roger. "She is not in your truck. But we know she is near here," said the man with the pale hair.

"Who is here?" asked Meggie.

"Carey-Lou is near here. We talked to a young man. His name was Cassidy. He said he saw Carey-Lou near this store yesterday," said one of the men.

"Carey-Lou? I don't know her. Go away. You are crazy men. I want to put my vegetables in the shed."

Winston ran out of the back of the supermarket.

"Help! Help!" he shouted. "A girl is taking food from my store! Call the police!"

"That's her!" shouted one of the men. They ran into the store.

Roger ran to the pile of boxes. "Quickly! Come now! You can hide in Meggie's truck."

Carey-Lou came out from behind the boxes. "I am too frightened."

"No! You must come. They are in the store, looking for you. You must be quick!"

Roger grabbed her arm and pulled her to the truck. He helped her climb in. "Hide behind the vegetables!"

Suddenly a van from Greenway Hardware came into the parking lot. Otis, Cameron and Oliver jumped out and ran into the store.

Winston, Meggie and Roger stood behind the truck and listened. There could hear shouting. They could hear the sound of breaking glass and falling cans.

"They're wrecking my store!" Winston was worried.

Then the Greenway brothers appeared. They were holding the men from Trayducket. Their arms were behind their backs, and the brothers were forcing them to walk towards their old truck. Their prisoners were kicking and biting, but Otis, Cameron and Oliver were too big and strong.

"Go now!" shouted Otis. "Or we will call the police."

The men got into their truck and drove away. As they left, one of them shouted out of the window. "Carey-Lou belongs to me! We'll be back!"

"You can come out now," called Roger.

Carey-Lou climbed out of the truck. She looked very, very young.

"Oh dear!" said Meggie. "I think we have a problem. In California, if young people are younger than eighteen, they can't leave home unless their parents agree. How old are you?"

"I was eighteen last week," said Carey-Lou.

"That's OK then. Now – who is going to help me unload the vegetables? Who is going to help Winston tidy his shop? It's a working day and we are all busy."

Everyone helped, and then the Greenways went back to their store.

"What are you going to do?" Roger asked Carey-Lou.

"I don't know. I am not safe in Chico. They will come back."

"You can come to my farm," said Meggie. "The cottage where Fionna is staying has two bedrooms. I hope you like cats. In a few days, we will make a plan. I think you should go to another state. The people from my church will help you."

Carey-Lou's eyes filled with tears. "You are all so kind."

Roger still had some questions. "How did you get here? Where is my bike?"

"Oh. I rode your bike to a truck stop. I hid there until a big truck came. While the man was inside drinking coffee I put the bike inside his truck and climbed in. I didn't care where I went. The first stop the truck made was here in Chico. Your bike is chained to a fence outside the post office. Here is the key. Your helmet is under the boxes next to the shed."

"Come now, Carey-Lou," said Meggie. "I have a lot to do today."

Carey-Lou hugged Roger. "Thank you," she said. Then she climbed into the passenger seat of the truck and Meggie drove away.

8. LEMONADE

Roger found his bike and his helmet. He stayed in Chico for a few more days. Ada Greenway recovered. She came back from her sister's house.

Roger packed his bags, said 'goodbye' to everyone and left to ride to Medford.

I will come back to see the Greenways, he thought. *I have met some great people – Meggie, Fionna, Anna, Winston and Carey-Lou. I don't think I will see Carey-Lou again. She must go far away. She must leave California.*

It took Roger three days to ride from Chico to Medford. He enjoyed the ride very much. He stayed in beautiful places and met some nice people, but he didn't have any more adventures.

Four months later, everyone in Medford was talking about the great new food truck. It was called 'Lemonade'. The menu was very interesting, the food was delicious and the coffee was good.

Roger and Kurt's new business was a success.

People sometimes asked why the food truck was called 'Lemonade'. Roger always laughed and pointed to an old calendar that hung inside the truck.

"I got the idea for this business from this old calendar - 'When life gives you lemons – make lemonade'. So that's what I did."

One day Roger got a letter from Cameron. *Why didn't he call or text me?* he wondered.

He opened the envelope. There was a note from Cameron and another envelope inside.

Cameron's note said ---*Mom and Dad are fine now, but Oliver and I plan to stay in Chico. Otis is getting married. Winston is retiring. He is selling the supermarket to Otis.*

I am sending you this letter from Carey-Lou. She sent it to Winston's supermarket, and Winston gave it to me.

Do you realise — after all that trouble, she didn't even know your name!

See you soon and good luck,

Cameron----

Roger looked at the other envelope and laughed. On the front of the envelope was written —- *To the man whose bike I stole in Butte City* —-

Inside he found a $20 note and a letter.

----Dear mystery man,

I am returning the money I stole from you. I hope you found your bike and it was OK.

Meggie, Fionna, and the people from their church were very good. They gave me clothes and money. They found me a job in Vermont. I look after children for a rich family. In the evenings I go to night school. When I have more education, I want to train to be a kindergarten teacher.

I hate the weather here. It is very cold. But I am pleased to be so far away from my grandfather, my cousin and the rest of my family. They will never find me here.

Thank you. You were so kind to me and you saved me from a very bad life. I changed my name because this is a new life and I wanted a new name. But I will never forget you.

Best wishes,
Carey-Lou James

THANK YOU

Thank you for reading Roger's Long Ride. (Word count: 7,896) We hope you enjoyed it.

If you would like to read more graded readers, please visit our website http://www.italkyoutalk.com

Other Level 3 graded readers include
A Dangerous Weekend
A Holiday to Remember
Akiko and Amy Part 1
Akiko and Amy Part 2
Akiko and Amy Part 3
Be My Valentine
Different Seas
Enjoy Your Business Trip
Enjoy Your Homestay
I'm Late!
I Need a Friend
Lincoln Takes a Trip
Match Day
Old Jack's Ghost Stories from England (1)
Old Jack's Ghost Stories from England (2)
Old Jack's Ghost Stories from Ireland
Old Jack's Ghost Stories from Japan
Old Jack's Ghost Stories from Scotland

Old Jack's Ghost Stories from Wales
Party Time!
Pretty and Bright
Rona
Stories for Christmas
Summer Days
The Curse
The Diary
Time to Go
Together Again
Who is Holly?
Wintertime

ABOUT THE AUTHOR

I Talk You Talk Press is an award-winning Japan-based publisher of language textbooks, graded readers and language learning/teaching resources. We won the Language Learner Literature Award in 2019 and 2020.

Our team is made up of highly experienced language teachers and translators, who have all studied at least one additional language to an advanced level.

This experience enables us to design our materials from the perspective of both the teacher and the learner. We consult with both teachers and language learners when designing our textbooks and graded readers, and test our materials extensively in the classroom before publication.

We are a fast-growing press, and currently publish graded readers for learners of English. We publish new graded readers monthly.